Think to Win

As you can guess, **The Fearless Girl and The Little Guy with Greatness: Think to Win** is all about empowering you to accomplish anything you set your mind to — anytime at any place.

In today's world, there are countless possibilities and ventures for you to take advantage of. That being the case, it is so incredibly important to have the right attitude and mindset in order to make the most of every opportunity.

This book is meant to serve as your guide towards achieving your goals and fulfilling your wildest dreams. We will cover a range of topics, including personal values, accountability, and integrity. Even more, you will learn the key ingredients to perseverance, which is fundamental to building a long, successful, and gratifying life.

At the end of each section, you will find a special "Try It Activity!" where you can practice becoming exceptional at thinking to win!

Written by

**Mort Greenberg &
Carly Greenberg**

Copyright © 2023 by
Mort Greenberg & Carly Greenberg

Design: Heri Susanto
Illustrations: Dian Kartika Abidin

First Paperback edition July 2023

ISBN 979-8-9880534-5-3

Published by TuckEmIn
www.tuckemin.com

Introduction

Tuck Em' In Publishing is a father and daughter effort that creates and publishes books for kids. Our mission is to Motivate and Inspire. Our vision is to help kids make the most of their todays and tomorrows.

The Fearless Girl and The Little Guy with Greatness is a book series that aims to share the following message: anything is possible for any kid if they put their mind to it.

Kids, you can find in our books ways to handle yourselves in important, real-life situations. Caregivers, you will find ways to push your kids to be their best selves. Through our books, we hope to encourage families to communicate more effectively with each other.

"Think to Win" is the fourth installment in The Fearless Girl and The Little Guy with Greatness series. The book will map out ten skills: (1) Values, (2) Accountability, (3) Integrity, (4) Mind-Body Connection, (5) Visualization, (6) Positive Self-Talk, (7) Toughness, (8) Never-Quit Mindset, (9) Flexibility, and (10) Continuous Learning — all of which are crucial for triumphant thinking.

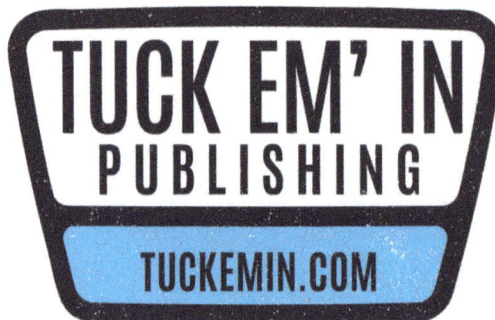

TUCK EM' IN PUBLISHING
TUCKEMIN.COM

Mort Greenberg and his daughter, Carly Greenberg, have embarked on numerous adventures together across the mountains of the United States. They also built self-guided, 18-hour day races in London, Paris, Milan, Venice, Murano, Burano, Rome, Buenos Aires, Tigre, Montevideo, Valparaiso, Santiago, Asuncion, and more.

This father and daughter team has worked through and overcome the same situations that you, as a parent, are experiencing now with a young daughter or son. Each skill in the book was inspired by an actual conversation that took place over the years from when Carly was five to ten years old.

This Book Belongs to

_____

Today's Date : _____

Sections (Table Of Contents)

Section 1

9

Values

In the simplest of words, **values are certain standards and principles that you hold in high regard.** Values influence people's thoughts and decisions, causing them to act one way or another.

Some values that you are already familiar with are honesty, kindness, and respect. All in all, your values serve as a general guide for your own behaviors.

Values can help you make good choices and live your life in a way that feels right. **When you act in accordance with your values, you feel happy and fulfilled.** When you go against your values, you feel guilty or unhappy.

For example, if you value honesty, you will feel bad after telling a lie. If you tell the truth, you will feel good and take pride in your actions.

Here are some examples of core values

Honesty
telling the truth and being trustworthy.

Respect
treating others with kindness and consideration.

Perseverance
staying committed to goals and working hard to achieve them.

Compassion
showing empathy and caring for others

Forgiveness
letting go of anger and resentment towards others.

Self-control
managing emotions and impulses to make good decisions.

Patience
being able to wait calmly and tolerate delays or difficulties.

99

Practicing your values means putting them into action in your everyday life. It is not always easy to live up to your values, but the more you practice, the easier it becomes."

Create a Values List

Make a list of 3 to 5 **values that are important to you**. You can write them down in a journal or just a blank sheet of paper.

15

Values Poster

Using the list, **create a poster that lists your core values**. Display it in your room once you're done. This way, you can look at the poster every day, and be reminded to practice those values.

Speak Up

If you see someone doing something that goes against your values, speak up. For example, if someone is bully-ing another person, don't stand idly by. Use your voice and let that bully know that their actions are wrong. **Use respectful language, but be firm in your beliefs.**

17

"

Values are an important part of who you are and how you operate in your daily life. By understanding your core values and living in accordance with them, you can build a strong foundation of integrity and character."

Section 2

Accountability

What does it mean to "take accountability"? Well, to put it plainly, it means to assume **responsibility for your actions**. When you take accountability, you are owning up to your mistakes and aiming to make things right. It's not typically an easy endeavor — fixing your wrongdoings — but by doing so, you demonstrate to others that you are indeed trustworthy and reliable.

Accountability also helps you to further **learn from your mistakes and grow as an individual.** When you take ownership of your actions, you are simultaneously identifying attributes of your character that require improvement. Once you've pinpointed those areas, you can figure out how to improve them.

To practice accountability, you must **be willing to admit fault**, even if it means there is a consequence. Think about it: before attempting to redeem the villain or save anyone, a hero must first determine what change is necessary within themselves. To be the best possible role model for others, you need to be your best self.

Reflect on Actions

Take time to reflect on your actions and their consequences. This can help you identify areas where you need to take on more responsibility. Maybe you upset your parents by failing to say "please" or "thank you." Or maybe you were being disruptive during class, and your teacher gave you a warning. Consider the consequences of those behaviors.

Keep Your Word

If you've made a promise, keep it. **This will show that you are reliable and trustworthy**. Perhaps you promised that you'd help a friend with their homework, or told a neighbor that you could watch their pet for a weekend. Make sure to follow through.

25

Make Things Right

When you've done something wrong, make things right. Apologize. **Take whatever actions are necessary in order to correct your mistakes**. It may be difficult, but sometimes, you just have to do it. From your efforts, something good is bound to come.

26

Section 3

Integrity

To have integrity means **consistently doing the right thing**. It doesn't matter if anyone is watching. In fact, it is about doing the right thing even when no one is watching. When you show integrity, you are demonstrating that you **value truth above all else.**

When you demonstrate strong moral principles and act honestly, you prove to others that you can be trusted and relied upon. By treating others with fairness and respect, you are showing that you value their feelings. In turn, others will be more likely to believe in you.

To practice integrity, you must be **sincere and uphold strong moral principles**. No matter what, make a conscious effort to act with honesty, fairness, and respect.

Practice Fairness

Look for opportunities to **be fair in your interactions with others**. As an example, when working on a group project at school, make sure that everyone's ideas are considered and discussed before making a decision. This way everyone that has contributed to the project earns credit for their efforts.

Tell the Truth

Always tell the truth, even if it's hard. This shows that you **value honesty and have integrity**. If you accidentally break something that belongs to someone else, it is important to tell the truth and admit what happened. This shows that you have integrity and respect for other people's property.

33

Treat Others with Respect

Always treat others with respect and fairness, even if you disagree with them. **Everyone is allowed to have their own opinions**, so it's all about compromise. It's your job to find the peace. This will show that you value others and have integrity.

Section 4

Mind-Body Connection

What exactly is the "mind-body connection"? It is the **way your thoughts and emotions affect your physical health and well-being**. For instance, when you feel happy and positive, your body tends to feel fit and energized. On the other hand, when you feel sad or stressed, your body might feel fatigued or sick.

The mind-body connection is important because it helps you understand that **your thoughts and emotions can have an impact** on your physical health and well-being. In a nutshell, your physical health improves when you look after your mental and emotional health, and vice versa.

So, what is the best way to take full advantage of the mind-body connection? The answer is simple: just take care of yourself. Understand that your thoughts and emotions have an impact on your physical well-being. If you're striving for success, you're going to have to be in the best physical, mental, and emotional state to do so

Positive Thinking

When life gets you down, **always remain positive**. Think about things that make you feel happy and grateful. Tell yourself that there are still countless exciting adventures to embark on.

40

Deep Breathing

Take deep breaths in and out. **Focus on your breathing**. This can help you feel more relaxed and calm when needed.

Physical Activity Challenge

If you enjoy dancing, turn up the radio and dance like nobody's watching. If you enjoy playing outside, put on some sneakers, grab a ball, and go soak up some sun. **Challenge yourself to do physical activities**. Your body will thank you for it.

42

Section 5

Visualization

Visualization is like making a movie in your mind. You are **imagining something you want to happen or achieve**, such as scoring a goal or giving a great presentation in class. You can envision what it looks like, sounds like, and even feels like.

Visualization is an amazing tactic for building confidence because it makes you feel more confident. When you visualize, you are **creating a mental picture of your success**, which can help you stay focused and motivated.

By imagining yourself doing something successfully, you will feel more equipped to take action. By picturing what you want clearly in your head, you will be more inspired to pursue it.

And when you put your heart and soul into something, your odds of success always increase.

Visualize

Close your eyes and **create a mental picture of something you want to achieve**, such as hitting a home run or performing in a school play. What does it look like? What does it sound like? What does it feel like?

47

Positive Affirmations

Use positive affirmations to reinforce your visualization.
Stand in front of the mirror, look at your reflection, and
tell yourself: **"I am confident and prepared for this. I can do
anything I set my mind to."**

48

Practice Regularly

Spend a few minutes every day visualizing yourself attaining your goals. The more you practice, the more you will improve. Here are some examples...

1

If your goal is to become a presenter in your classroom, visualize yourself delivering a confident and engaging speech. See yourself standing tall, making eye contact, and commanding the attention of your friends.

49

2 **If you're training for a race**, visualize yourself crossing the finish line. Imagine the feeling of accomplishment you will have as you approach the end of the race, and the cheers of the crowd.

3 **If your goal is to improve your guitar playing**, see yourself strumming the chords with ease, moving seamlessly between notes, and feeling the music flow through you.

Section 6

Positive-Self-Talk

Self-talk is precisely what you think it is. It is the way you mentally talk to yourself. Think of it as having a voice inside your head that can impact you positively or negatively. **When you talk to yourself in a positive way, you feel good and become more competent.** When you talk to yourself in a negative way, you lose the edge you otherwise will have. So always choose to talk to yourself in a positive way!

Have you ever thought negatively about yourself? Have you ever thought "I'm not good enough" or "I can't do this"? If you have, then it is important that you practice positive self talk. In other words, it is time for you to start changing those negative thoughts into positive ones!

Positive self-talk helps you feel better about yourself and it encourages you to look on "the bright side" of things. By talking to yourself positively — pumping yourself up with affirmations like "I can do this!" or "I am smart and capable!" — you gain an edge and build up your confidence to be your best self.

I am going to
be the best

Use Positive Language

Use positive language when talking to yourself and others. Stop saying "I can't." Instead, tell yourself **"I will give it my best shot"**, **"I am going to be the best"**, **"I've got this"**, **"this is mine"**, or **"time to do the work and win"**.

Positive Notes

Write a **positive note to yourself**. Leave it somewhere you will see it often, such as a phone case or in your backpack.

Mirror Talk

Come up with a list of **3 positive things about yourself**. Stand in front of a mirror and say those compliments sincerely to your reflection. They can be as specific as **"I am a good artist"** or as broad as **"I am loved by my friends and family."** Repeat these affirmations several times, and take note of how you feel afterwards.

57

I never give up!

Here are a few suggestions to help get you started:

"**I am a great problem-solver**! Whenever I face a difficult challenge, I always find a way to overcome it."

"**I am a hard worker** who always gives my best effort. Even when things get tough, I never give up!"

"**I am unique and special**. There is no one else like me in the world, and that makes me valuable."

"**I am adaptable and flexible**. I can handle changes and adjust my plans as needed."

58

Section 7

Never-Quit Mindset

A never-quit mindset means that, despite how **difficult** something seems, you **keep on trying**. It is all about being persistent. When you have a never-quite mindset, you **refuse to give up.**

Developing a never quit mindset is essential to raising your resilience. As you continue to grow, you will find yourself facing obstacles. Because of this, it is best to strengthen your resolve so that you can **endure and overcome whatever life throws at you.**

When you don't give up, not only do you demonstrate that you are capable of handling difficult situations, but you also teach yourself the art of bouncing back. With enough determination, every problem can be solved.

To practice a never-quit mindset is to **never raise the white flag and surrender.** Even when things get hard, keep on trying. Keep seeking out another alternative.

Learn from Mistakes

When you make a mistake, learn from it. Identify what you did wrong and **look for ways to improve**.

Set Goals

Set **realistic goals** for yourself and actively
work towards achieving them.

Practice Perseverance

Keep on trying. If you are dead-set on achieving something, never give up. **Everything is attainable if you put your mind to it.**

Section 8

Toughness

Toughness is defined as **being strong and resilient**. It is a direct companion of the never-quit mindset, helping you to further reinforce and harden your durability.

Toughness is important because it makes you that much more capable of achieving your desired goals. It helps you up so that you can go head-to-head with the most difficult challenges that you face.

Even when the tides threaten to knock you down, toughness will keep your feet fixed on the ground.

Even more, toughness can also help you to **improve your overall confidence and self-esteem.** Consider this: when you overcome a challenge, don't you feel proud of yourself? Don't you feel more reassured of your abilities? That's the monumental effect of toughness and a never-quit mindset!

To practice toughness is to **clench your fists and hold your head up high**. It means to never succumb to pressure or steer your eyes away from something you really want. Setbacks are inevitable, but so is bouncing back!

Face Challenges

Search for opportunities to challenge yourself, such as trying a new sport or learning a new skill. When you attempt something new, you start at ground zero. Nevertheless, as you undergo various trials, **you learn how to cope with both success and failure**. This, in turn, will help you build resilience and toughness.

Take Risks

Don't be afraid to take healthy risks. **Be bold and step out of your comfort zone.** Every risk taken develops your courage, thus transforming you into a force to be reckoned with.

73

Support Others

It is also important to support
others as they too face challenges.
Lend a hand to those who may need a
mental or physical boost. On top of helping
you develop empathy and compassion, such
gestures will also fortify your own toughness.

74

Section 9

Flexibility

Flexibility is the **ability to adapt to change**. It is about being open-minded and willing to try out new things. Flexibility is a trait that can take some practice, but once understood will help you soar to victory all of the time.

77

When you are inflexible you limit what is possible. When you are flexible, you **expand your horizons, allowing yourself to experience life in a brand-new way.**

For instance, when you learn how to ride a bike, you gain the freedom to travel at a faster pace. When you are flexible, you become unstoppable.

Flexibility also enhances your capacity for empathy. By broadening your mind, you improve your understanding and acceptance of others. As a result, you can connect with people from different backgrounds.

For example, when you study a second language you give yourself the power to communicate in a new way and make new friends.

To practice flexibility is to **learn how to bend and flow with a situation.** Change can be complicated — and can take time — but it is a worthwhile investment in your future self. That's why it is important to open up your mind to other ways of doing something, and embrace being flexible.

Adapt to Changes

When something changes, such as a schedule or plan, try to **adapt and find a new solution**. This will help you become more flexible and adaptable.

80

Embrace Differences

Embrace differences in people, cultures, and ideas. This will help you **become more agreeable and accepting**.

81

Try New Things

Try new foods, activities, or hobbies. This will help
you become **more flexible and open-minded**.

Section 10

Continuous Learning

Continuous learning means always seeking out new knowledge and skills. It's about being curious and interested in learning new things, even outside of school.

If you want to truly grow and develop as an individual, continuous learning is pivotal. Think of it this way: **the more information you learn, the more resources you can make use of in the future.**

By constantly seeking out new knowledge and skills, you supplement your flexibility so that you can adeptly adapt to given any situation.

To practice continuous learning is to be constantly on the hunt for the unknown. **Take advantage of every opportunity to discover something new.** It's about developing a love of learning that exceeds the classroom. The world is full of hidden gems. You just need to go out and find them.

Read Books

Read books about **topics that catch
your attention**, such as animals,
sports, travel, science, or history.

88

Research Project

Choose a topic that interests
you and **research it using books
or the internet.**

89

Skill-Building Activity

Choose a skill you'd like to learn. Perhaps you're interested in cooking, drawing, language, gymnastics, or martial arts. **Make an effort to practice that skill regularly.**

Conclusion

Congratulations! You've gained valuable insights and strategies for accomplishing anything. By mastering these skills and traits, you are sure to build a strong foundation for success and fulfillment in all areas of your life.

Remember: With the right mindset, you can overcome any obstacle. So, continue learning, growing, and striving for greatness. Embrace continuous learning and improvement, and never give up on your dreams.

Smart Money Moves

About The Authors

For the past 25 years **Mort Greenberg** has been a salesperson and sales manager for technology start-ups and larger media companies. Fighting his way up from an Account Executive to a role as a division President you can guess there were many challenges that needed to be overcome. Along the way Mort launched two companies, FitAd and MindFlight and learned many hard-fought lessons that start-ups are not always successful. He is a graduate of the State University of New York at New Paltz where he studied International Relations and Economics. While in college he started a company selling screen printing and promotional items to local businesses and on-campus organizations. At the same time, he also volunteered as a Congressional District Intern for the U.S. House of Representatives. He is an Eagle Scout and in junior high school bought several newspaper routes from neighborhood kids to create his first business. Mort is also the author of the *Revenue Vs. Sales*, a three book series that you can find on Amazon.com.

Carly Greenberg attends the University of Maryland's Smith School of Business with a double major in marketing and management. Carly's twin brother has autism, and she has helped him find his voice through her unique interactions with him. He is the original little guy with greatness. Carly is the original fearless girl, always helping others, volunteering, and finding ways to do more with less - all while having to put up with a crazy dad. Carly also holds a black belt in Tae Kwon Do.

www.ingramcontent.com/pod-product-compliance
Lightning Source LLC
Chambersburg PA
CBHW052343210326
41597CB00037B/6245